W9-CIP-529

NUMBERS 1–20

Know Your Numbers

NATURE

Mary Elizabeth Salzmann

Consulting Editor, Diane Craig, M.A./Reading Specialist

Sandcastle

An Imprint of Abdo Publishing
www.abdopublishing.com

visit us at www.abdopublishing.com

Published by Abdo Publishing, a division of ABDO, PO Box 398166, Minneapolis, Minnesota 55439. Copyright © 2015 by Abdo Consulting Group, Inc. International copyrights reserved in all countries. No part of this book may be reproduced in any form without written permission from the publisher. SandCastle™ is a trademark and logo of Abdo Publishing.

Printed in the United States of America, North Mankato, Minnesota
062014
092014

Editor: Alex Kuskowski
Content Developer: Nancy Tuminelly
Cover and Interior Design: Anders Hanson, Mighty Media, Inc.
Photo Credits: Shutterstock

Library of Congress Cataloging-in-Publication Data
Salzmann, Mary Elizabeth, 1968- author.
  Know your numbers. Nature / Mary Elizabeth Salzmann.
     pages cm. -- (Numbers 1-20)
  Audience: Ages 3-9.
  ISBN 978-1-62403-266-0
1. Counting--Juvenile literature. 2. Cardinal numbers--Juvenile literature. 3. Nature--Juvenile literature. I. Title. II. Title: Nature.
  QA113.S294 2015
  513.2--dc23
                          2013041912

SandCastle™ Level: Beginning

SandCastle™ books are created by a team of professional educators, reading specialists, and content developers around five essential components—phonemic awareness, phonics, vocabulary, text comprehension, and fluency—to assist young readers as they develop reading skills and strategies and increase their general knowledge. All books are written, reviewed, and leveled for guided reading, early reading intervention, and Accelerated Reader® programs for use in shared, guided, and independent reading and writing activities to support a balanced approach to literacy instruction. The SandCastle™ series has four levels that correspond to early literacy development. The levels are provided to help teachers and parents select appropriate books for young readers.

EMERGING · **BEGINNING** · TRANSITIONAL · FLUENT

Contents

There is 1 caterpillar on the branch.
It will become a **butterfly**.

· = 1 = one

1 2 3 4 5 6 7 8 9 10 11 12 13 14 15 16 17 18 19 20

Mushrooms grow in the forest.
There are 2 mushrooms.

●● = 2 = two

The nest has 3 bird's eggs.
The eggs are blue.

●●● = 3 = three

1 2 3 4 5 6 7 8 9 10 11 12 13 14 15 16 17 18 19 20

Charles found a lucky **clover**!
It has 4 leaves.

●●●● = 4 = four

1 2 3 **4** 5 6 7 8 9 10 11 12 13 14 15 16 17 18 19 20

7

There are 5 **palm** trees.
They grow in Florida.

●●●●● = 5 = five

1 2 3 4 **5** 6 7 8 9 10 11 12 13 14 15 16 17 18 19 20

The turtles sit on a log.
There are 6 turtles.

●●●●●● = 6 = six

1 2 3 4 5 6 7 8 9 10 11 12 13 14 15 16 17 18 19 20

Kate has 7 **acorns**.
Acorns come from oak trees.

⬤⬤⬤⬤⬤ = 7 = seven

1 2 3 4 5 6 7 8 9 10 11 12 13 14 15 16 17 18 19 20

There are 8 tulips.
Tulips **bloom** in the spring.

 = 8 = eight

There are 9 ears of Indian corn.
It is also called flint corn.

●●●●● ●●●● = 9 = nine

1 2 3 4 5 6 7 8 9 10 11 12 13 14 15 16 17 18 19 20

There are 10 pieces of **quartz**.
Quartz comes from **underground**.

= 10 = ten

Baby ducks are called ducklings.
The mother duck has 11 ducklings.

●●●●●
●●●●●● = 11 = eleven

1 2 3 4 5 6 7 8 9 10 **11** 12 13 14 15 16 17 18 19 20

14

The feet were made with 12 rocks.
They are on the beach.

= 12 = twelve

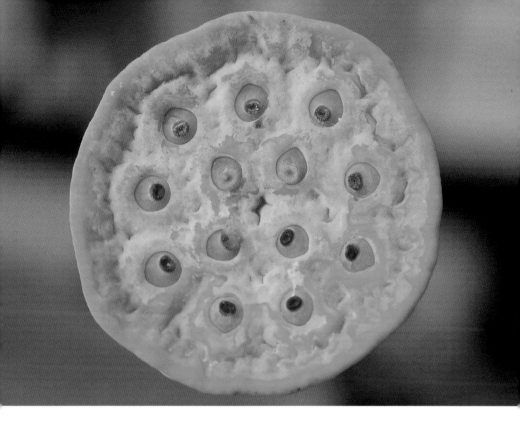

Lotus seeds grow in a pod.
This pod has 13 seeds.

= 13 = thirteen

1 2 3 4 5 6 7 8 9 10 11 12 **13** 14 15 16 17 18 19 20

Robert throws leaves in the air.
There are 14 leaves.

 = 14 = fourteen

1 2 3 4 5 6 7 8 9 10 11 12 13 **14** 15 16 17 18 19 20

The fish swim in the ocean.
There are 15 fish.

You can find seashells on the beach.
There are 16 seashells.

 = 16 = sixteen

1 2 3 4 5 6 7 8 9 10 11 12 13 14 15 **16** 17 18 19 20

These pinecones are from pine trees.
There are 17 pinecones.

= 17 = seventeen

1 2 3 4 5 6 7 8 9 10 11 12 13 14 15 16 **17** 18 19 20

There are 18 white feathers.
They are soft.

 = 18 = eighteen

The leaf is wet with dew.
There are 19 dewdrops.

⊞ = 19 = nineteen

1 2 3 4 5 6 7 8 9 10 11 12 13 14 15 16 17 18 **19** 20

Icicles form in the winter.
There are 20 icicles.

= 20 = twenty

Glossary

acorn – the seed from an oak tree.

bloom – to produce flowers.

butterfly – a thin insect with large, brightly colored wings.

clover – a small plant that has three or four leaves, and pink or white flowers.

icicle – a hanging point of ice formed when dripping water freezes.

lotus – a flowering plant that grows in water.

mushroom – an umbrella-shaped fungus. Some mushrooms are used in cooking.

palm – a tall tree whose leaves are all at the top and that grows in warm places.

quartz – a hard, common mineral that can be clear or brightly colored.

underground – below the surface of the earth.